D0581935

LATERAL THINKING PUZZLES

THIS IS A CARLTON BOOK

Published in 2016 by Carlton Books Limited
an imprint of the Carlton Publishing Group
20 Mortimer Street
London W1T 3JW

A catalogue record for this book is available from the
British Library

ISBN 978-1-78097-832-1

Printed in Dubai

10 9 8 7 6 5

LATERAL THINKING
PUZZLES

MORE THAN 90 BRAINTEASERS
TO SOLVE WITH LOGICAL REASONING

ERWIN BRECHER, PhD

CARLTON
BOOKS

CONTENTS

ABOUT THE AUTHOR

Erwin Brecher was educated in Vienna, Czechoslovakia and London. He studied physics, economics and engineering to become AMIMechE and AMIProdE. For his PhD, he majored in psychology. Brecher joined the Czech army in 1937, and at the outbreak of war escaped to London via Switzerland. He worked for De Havilland on aircraft design, and in 1946 formed a group of companies active in international trade and finance. In 1963 his companies were acquired by a listed investment trust. He was appointed to the main board and to the board of its banking subsidiary. In 1972 Erwin Brecher became CEO of an international financial group with offices in New York, Rio de Janeiro, Switzerland, Athens and Istanbul. He specialized in developing a technique known as International Counter-trade in connection with which he travelled extensively. In 1974 he became a Name at Lloyds of London. Then in 1978, he acquired control of a quoted investment trust and served as its chairman until his retirement in 1984. Erwin Brecher was a shareholder and on the board of MBA International, a specialist recruitment company. He was also CEO of a company of financial consultants (established in 1947).

He was the author of many books on non-fiction subjects, published in six languages by US and European companies. In September 1995 he was awarded the Order of Merit in Gold by the city of Vienna in recognition of his literary achievements.

Erwin Brecher was a member of Mensa and has been a regular contributor to magazines and radio.

INTRODUCTION

This book deals with a novel and exciting approach to puzzle-solving, describing situations which appear unusual and even weird, defying any attempt to find a ready explanation. However, the puzzles are constructed in a manner which will make the circumstances fit one reasonable and logical answer. Each puzzle contains, in addition to irrelevancies, all necessary ingredients to satisfy the solution.

While solving these puzzles is usually quite tough, creating new ones along similar lines need not be, once players have developed an understanding of what makes them tick. Devotees should therefore be able to keep the parlour game going after the examples provided in this book are exhausted. Indeed I am looking forward to a flood of ideas from my readers, which will be gratefully acknowledged.

Strange situations, by their very nature, appear to provide the possibility of more than just one correct answer. Indeed, at first glance they might seem to offer an almost infinite number of solutions, limited only by the breadth of the solver's imagination. Certainly, they do not have mathematically definitive answers in the way that conventional puzzles do; but in my experience, on both sides of the fence, there is usually only one solution – ignoring minor variations of detail – that both puzzler and responder find correct and satisfactory.

Substantially different alternatives tend to seem second-rate, even to the answerers who devized them, once the "official" answer is known.

As to the technique of interrogation, finding the solution requires a radically different thought process from the standard puzzle. The issues in most conventional brain-teasers are self-evident; they jump out at the puzzler and trigger the thought processes, leading in a direction (which may turn out to be right or wrong). For instance, if a problem requires calculation with pen and paper, the puzzler is usually able to begin the figure work and put pen to paper as soon as he or she has finished reading it. This is not the case with the problems in this book.

They are conundrums in which half the battle is figuring out where to begin and which piece of given information is the key to unravelling the mystery. They test a kind of cross between lateral and intuitive thinking rather than mechanical intelligence, numeracy or acquired knowledge.

The problems are generally in the form of a narrative, telling a story that seems out of kilter in some way. It may seem wildly improbable or contradictory; it may describe bizarre or otherwise inexplicable conduct; it may even seem to defy the laws of physics! But there is a rational explanation for the story and the object of the puzzle is to find that explanation.

The ground rules are as follows: The solution must obviously fit all the given facts, must conform to accepted norms of behaviour and obey the laws of the physical world as we know it; in other words, you can take it for granted that none of the solutions involves women from Mars who can fly and see through concrete.

Having said that, perhaps I should add one thing. By "rational explanation" I do not mean to suggest that the situations, once explained, will all seem realistic in everyday-world terms, merely that they will suddenly make sense according to the puzzler's concept of acceptable logic.

Happy puzzling!

Erwin Brecher

PLAYING AS A GAME

Although you can of course tackle these problems on your own, they can also be great fun as a parlour game, which is best played with a moderator who knows the answer, and one or several participants who can ask any number of questions which the moderator can only answer with "Yes" or "No" until one of the players has found the solution. A useful refinement is to add "Irrelevant" to the moderator's responses, as many questions cannot be answered with "Yes" or "No" and to do so would only confuse the questioner. As an alternative to one or more individuals playing the game, the participants (if more than three) can split into two groups, who are permitted to consult among themselves.

There are many puzzles with complex solutions, which can be arrived at only in stages, in which case the participants profit substantially from questions and answers of competitors. It is therefore advizable to base the scoring on an aggregate of questions yielding a "Yes" response and awarding bonus points to the group, which articulates the correct solution. Two points are awarded for asking a correct question about the background and 10 points for finding the solution. If just one person is playing alone, then take away 1 point for each question asked, right or wrong, but give 20 points for the correct answer.

The key to success is an intelligent and methodical approach to formulating questions, which should be designed to narrow the field in successive steps, almost like a forensic exercise.

Let us take one of the classic riddles and see how it works:

A banker lives on the twentieth floor of a high-rise apartment building in Manhattan. Each morning when he goes to work he calls the lift, pushes the ground-floor button and is driven by chauffeured limousine to his Wall Street office.

On his return home he enters the lift, usually pushes the twelfth-floor button and walks up the rest of the stairs. At other times he rides straight up to his floor.

Question – Why does he not always take the lift to the twentieth floor?

Assuming two teams, Team A and Team B, the game and the scoring might develop something like this:

> **Team A**: Is there a regular pattern in the banker's behaviour?
> Answer: No.
> **Team B**: Does he walk up for exercise?
> Answer: No.
> **Team A**: Does he occasionally visit someone on the twelfth floor? Answer: No.
> **Team B**: Is his behaviour random?
> Answer: No.

Team A: Is going to the twelfth or twentieth floor conditional on extraneous circumstances?
Answer: Yes, +2 Bonus Points.
Team B: Are other people involved in his decision?
Answer: Yes, +2 Bonus Points.
Team A: Are these people also travelling in the lift with him? Answer: Yes, +2 Bonus Points.
Team B: Are the other passengers also stopping on the twelfth floor? Answer: Irrelevant.
Team A: Does he stop at the twelfth floor only if there are no other passengers in the lift?
Answer: Yes, +2 Bonus Points.
Team B: Is he disabled?
Answer: No.
Team A: Is he for any reason unable to operate the twentieth-floor button?
Answer: Yes, + 2 Bonus Points.
Team B: Is he very short?
Answer: Yes, 10 points.
Team B wins by 12 points to 8.

PUZZLES

THE ASSASSIN

It was midnight when Joan and Eric arrived home. They had just got out of the car when a man stepped out of shadowy bushes nearby and shot Eric at close range. Eric slumped to the ground. The man fired one more shot, as if to ensure that his victim was dead, and walked away unhurriedly. Joan collapsed in shock and was taken to her house by a neighbour who had heard the shots. She was still under sedation when she was questioned by the police the next morning.

The investigation into the affair had produced evidence of Eric's involvement with organized crime in his early days. Furthermore, Joan was found to be the sole beneficiary of a substantial insurance policy on Eric's life. Her relationship with the neighbour was also unusually close. It was therefore not surprizing that Joan was considered a prime suspect.

Furthermore, during questioning, Joan had given a very detailed description of the assassin, which subsequently proved to be completely false. Yes, Joan had deliberately tried to mislead the police, yet neither she nor her neighbour was involved in the homicide. In fact, Joan had been very devoted to her husband. Why, then, did she mislead the police?

BLUE EYES

Karen Selby loved her job. She was head stewardess in the first-class section of Pan-Am's London-New York-London route. On a beauty scale of 1 to 10 her rating would vary depending on the personal taste of the judge between 8 and 9. It is therefore no surprise that she had many offers from adoring passengers, ranging from one-night stands to long weekends and, in the extreme, two proposals of marriage.

However, following company policy, Karen was immune to all entreaties, even to dinner invitations with no strings attached. But she had one fatal obsession: Karen was unable to resist a man with blue eyes.

I suppose it was bound to happen one day. On Christmas Eve on Karen's last trip of the year, there were just three first-class passengers. One of them, Ronnie Steiner, had the bluest eyes she had ever seen. It was instant meltdown, and all Karen could do was to pray that he would ask her out. Ronnie, engrossed in his book, did not seem to notice her, but when they disembarked he looked at her with a frivolous smile and asked her to have dinner with him. The rest is history. They got married and for three years it was paradise. Then disaster struck and Ronnie left her.

When the divorce papers arrived she was devastated. It took more than a year for her to recover and take another job, as switchboard operator for the Metalex Corporation. There were a number of regular callers, and Karen soon recognized their voices. One of them, Eric Morgan, meant more to her than all the others. He had a sexy, mellifluous voice, and whenever he announced himself her heart missed a beat. Eric seemed to be equally attracted because he often telephoned not to be connected but just to speak to her.

The inevitable happened. They fell in love over the telephone. However, when he asked her to meet him, she refused and broke down in tears. In fact, she was so distraught that she resigned from her job and never spoke to Eric again.

Why?

THE LINE-UP

Jean Brody was just leaving the Midland Bank branch in
Cricklewood when a man on a motorbike stopped in front
of her. Without uttering a word, he cut the leather strap of
her handbag and sped away. Jean was most upset as her bag
contained £2,000 in £50 notes, all her credit cards and, most
worrying, the keys to her flat. However, while she did not
remember the registration number of the bike, she could give
an accurate description of the assailant to the police officer to
whom she reported the incident.

True enough, a man answering her description was arrested a
few hours later. The police needed positive identification and Jean
Brody had no difficulty in picking out the man in a line-up of six.

At the court hearing the prosecutor looked demonstratively at
his watch as if to say, 'What a waste of time.' The defendant had
previous convictions, owned a motorbike, was arrested in the
vicinity, and after all was clearly identified by the victim. If ever
there was an open-and-shut case, this was it.

The defending counsel rose slowly from his seat. He asked only
for a photograph to be taken in evidence and when this was
shown to the judge and the jury, the prosecution was laughed out
of court. The judge, hardly containing his mirth, instructed the
jury to dismiss the charge.

Can you find an explanation?

THE BLUE MOVIE

Stephen Kelly was leaving a restaurant in London's Soho when he was accosted by a scruffy-looking man, obviously a tout. The following conversation ensued:

> Tout: (whispering) Would you like to see a hard-porn blue movie?

> Stephen: OK, but how much will you pay me to see it?

> Tout: (with some agitation) You don't understand, you have to pay me to see it.

> Stephen: My good man, it is you who do not understand. You have to pay me, but I will be reasonable.

Was Stephen joking?

WALKING TO
THE PARK

Eric Black left his apartment in New York each morning at precisely 8 a.m. for his daily walk in Central Park. Passers-by smiled as he walked down the street because his walk, with its strange, exaggerated steps, resembled something straight out of the "Ministry of Silly Walks" from the Monty Python shows. However, as soon as he arrived at the park his walk became perfectly normal.

Explain.

THE DIALOGUE

The last customer had left, and the High Street branch of First National Credit Bank was just about to close for the day when a well-dressed man entered the premises. His face was covered by a balaclava with only his eyes showing. In his left hand he held a Marks & Spencer's carrier bag, and as he approached the counter he shoved a piece of paper across to the cashier and mumbled, "No fifties."

Tom, the security man who was just about to pack up, turned round and approached cautiously with his hand on the holster of his gun. At that moment Elsa, the cashier, exchanged a few words with the masked man. Hearing the dialogue, Tom withdrew without uttering a word. The man stuffed the notes into the carrier bag and left unhurriedly.

Strangely enough, neither Elsa nor Tom phoned the police as soon as they were alone, nor did the bank submit a claim, although they were well insured. Can you guess what happened?

MURDER IN THE FAMILY

There was a loud knock at the door late one Sunday evening at the home of William and Janet Garner. William answered the door to a man who introduced himself as Detective Greg Nelson of the Los Angeles Police Department and informed William, "I'm afraid that your brother-in-law was found brutally murdered this afternoon." William gasped, "Oh my god! Poor Ben! Who could have done such a terrible thing? My wife will be devastated."

William invited Detective Nelson inside and went to awaken his wife Janet, who had gone to bed early with a headache. When Janet heard the news, she became hysterical and the doctor was called to administer a sedative. Detective Nelson asked them to come to his office the following morning to make statements.

When William and Janet arrived at police headquarters the following morning, they were shown into Greg Nelson's office. "Have either of you any idea as to who had a motive?" Nelson asked. "It certainly appears that Ben knew his killer."

William looked over at Janet, "There's my sister Elizabeth's husband, Arthur. He's a really weird guy and has threatened Ben during the many arguments they've had." Janet wiped away the tears that were rolling down her cheeks and said quietly, "There's my other brother – Peter – but he and Ben were very close. In any case, Peter is out of town at the moment."

William leaned forward in his seat: "Of course, there is Uncle Lawrence. He always said that Ben wished him dead so that he could get his hands on his money and he was convinced that Ben was trying to kill him. Come to think of it, cousin Philip owed Ben a lot of money and Ben threatened him with violence if he didn't pay up."

"I've heard enough," interjected Inspector Nelson. "It's obvious to me that you, William Garner, committed the murder and I am placing you under arrest." How did Inspector Nelson come to this conclusion?

THE WEEKEND PARTY

To say that life is stranger than fiction is considered a cliché, but even so it is often true. It happened after a party in a Leicestershire country estate.

Joan and her boyfriend Fred who lived in Stockport were invited and given one of the ornate, if old-fashioned bedroom suites for their stay. The party lasted the whole weekend and was a delightful affair. Catering was superb and the congenial atmosphere turned the get-together of old friends into an unforgettable experience.

On Monday morning most guests had departed, and Joan and Fred prepared for their journey home. Having finished their packing, Joan looked around as if searching for something. She finally turned to Fred and asked jokingly: "You haven't by any chance drunk the glass of water on the dressing table?" Fred nodded and all of a sudden – pandemonium!

Joan had to phone the Automobile Association's rescue service. Less than an hour later an AA man arrived, hitched her car to his breakdown van and towed the embarrassed couple home, where they arrived after a two-and-a-half hour journey.

What do you think had happened?

09

DRIVE CAREFULLY

It happened on a main road in a built-up area with a speed limit of 30 miles per hour. A white Rolls-Royce Corniche was speeding at 80 miles per hour through the village, hitting a pedestrian who was crossing the road, throwing him to the roadside where he lay, bleeding profusely, until an ambulance arrived.

Although there were several witnesses about who noted the car's number and could testify as to the speed, the driver was not prosecuted, even though his identity could be easily ascertained.

Explain.

10

LUXURY CRUISE

It is easy to turn travel companions into friends during a transatlantic crossing, but such friendships seldom survive the five days from Southampton to New York.

The following took place during the third evening on the *Queen Mary*. After dinner and a few rounds of bridge, a small but select group gathered for drinks and small talk at the bar on the promenade deck. The group included a real-estate tycoon – Robert Waterman – and his young secretary Madame Croiseau and her toy-boy, plus Count Orlando and his beautiful wife Elisabeth. Fred Gerrard, the renowned jeweller, was entertaining the party with stories of famous diamonds and their fate.

In the rough, the great Mogul found in 1650 in India weighed 787 carats. The Orloff was stolen by a French soldier, bought by Prince Orloff and given to Catherine The Great of Russia. The most famous of them all, the Koh-i-nor, changed hands many times and was acquired by the British in 1849. Possibly the most fascinating story concerned the affair of the diamond necklace, the scandal at the court of Louis XVI in 1785, which discredited the French monarchy and, according to Napoleon, was one of the major causes of the French Revolution.

The conversation then turned to the high cost of insuring precious stones. To solve the problem, jewels were kept in a bank vault and instead replicas were worn by the owners. Waterman was of the opinion that these imitations were of such excellent quality that only the closest expert examination would discover the fake. Fred Gerrard begged to differ and maintained that the trained eye would know the difference at arm's length. This statement was met with disbelief by everyone.

To prove his point, Gerrard looked at Madame Croiseau's diamond bracelet and without hesitation described it as a superb imitation. To alleviate her obvious embarrassment, he added, "Madame, I am sure that the real thing is safe and sound in the ship's vault." A slight nod from Madame confirmed his diagnosis. The round of subdued applause acknowledged the expertize.

"On the other hand," he continued, "the Countess's necklace is one of the most exquisite pieces of jewellery I have seen for some time." The Countess visibly blushed and looked at Gerrard with a strange expression. The Count smiled with obvious satisfaction. "This time you are mistaken, dear boy." "Impossible," retorted the jeweller. "Would you care to wager, say $500?" said the Count. Gerrard accepted, and the Countess handed him the necklace for closer examination. He looked at it for a few seconds and then glanced at the Countess. "You win,"

he said to the Count, handing him the amount wagered. The party broke up and everyone returned to their cabins.

Next morning Gerrard noticed a piece of paper that had been slipped under his cabin door. On it was a lipstick mark and the words "Thank you."

Explain.

11

THE GLOBETROTTER

I know of a man who, as part of his profession, regularly has to visit 80 foreign countries. He does so in a single day, is welcomed everywhere, and enters and leaves without going through Customs or Immigration. Surprizingly, he does not even hold a passport.

Who is he?

12

THE
CONTRACTORS

A true story. A man designed plans for an extension to his property. He approached several builders for quotations to cover the work involved. He received three quotes at about the same price. However, a fourth offered to build the extension free of charge.

Why would he do that?

ATTICA

The prisoners were assembled in the mess hall for dinner. Two of the most feared inmates, Jaime Sanchez and Moses Washington, were engaged in a heated discussion about the spiralling violence between their rival factions.

Both men had started their adult life with great promise. Jaime's parents always thought that their son would follow his father into the medical profession and had spared no expense to put him through medical school. Things started to go very wrong when

Jaime began to take drugs, and very soon he was completely out of control, becoming involved in drug-pushing and eventually murder.

Moses, on the other hand, had trained to be a priest but had allowed himself to be influenced by his old friends, who were all members of street gangs. Very soon his religious vocation went out of the window and he became even more vicious and ruthless than the rest of the gang. Moses glared maliciously across the table at Jaime and called him a vile name. Jaime responded by making crude comments about Moses' parents. Suddenly Moses' face turned purple and he gripped Jaime's arm like a vice. Jaime immediately struck Moses a fearful blow with his fist, then produced from somewhere a vicious-looking handmade knife and stuck it into Moses, who fell forward onto the table, bleeding profusely. The guards quickly moved in and Moses was rushed to the infirmary.

The next day Jaime was brought to visit Moses in the hospital. When Moses saw Jaime he took him warmly by the hand, thanked him and promised that he would never call him names again.

Explain.

14

THE COLLISION

Henry was a happy man. He had just signed a contract for the supply of 3,000 tons of fertilizer to the Agricultural Cooperative of Maryland. Driving along the busy freeway at some speed in his old Chevrolet, Henry was trying to work out his profit on the deal and toying with the idea of replacing his clapped-out car with a new Cadillac.

He was so absorbed in his thoughts that he was not paying attention to the road. His car veered from its lane, collided with six vehicles in the adjacent lane and overturned. Henry and the driver of one of the other vehicles were killed instantly.

The other cars involved in the carnage were complete write-offs. However, no other driver was killed, injured or even scratched.

Were they just lucky?

15

THE PARROT

It was now six months since Gertrude James had lost her husband, and living alone with only memories and no one to talk to had made her very depressed. One day she decided she would get herself a pet to keep her company. After looking around the local pet store, she could not make up her mind whether to get a dog or a cat. "Why not get a parrot?" the pet-shop manager suggested. Why not? she thought, I could teach it to speak and then I would at least have someone to talk to. "Does this parrot speak?" she asked the shopkeeper. "This parrot, madam, will repeat every word it hears, I can assure you," replied the shopkeeper. Gertrude promptly bought the parrot and took it home.

Three months later, after trying almost constantly to get the parrot to speak, Gertrude could not get it to utter one word. Can you come up with an explanation, assuming the shopkeeper spoke the truth?

PILGRIMAGE

A man left home on Monday, riding a donkey, to make a pilgrimage to Canterbury. The journey took two days. He stayed two days in Canterbury. The journey home took another two days. He arrived home on Friday.

How?

THE MURDER

It was a busy morning in the city. On a fifth-floor terrace of a brownstone in Manhattan, two men were seen to quarrel viciously. A crowd in the street below watched the scene with morbid interest.

Suddenly, one of the men took hold of the other's legs and tossed him over the balustrade. The victim hit the street with a crushing thud and died shortly thereafter. Strangely, it was one of the onlookers and not the man who had attacked the victim, who was eventually indicted.

Why?

18

THE ACCIDENT

On a frosty winter morning, Farmer Jones was walking with
his dog through the snow-covered field adjoining his stables.
Suddenly, the dog started to bark excitedly, pulling him toward a
lonely tree in the middle of the field. It was then that the farmer
spotted a man hanging from the tree. The second thing that the
observant Jones noticed was that the snow in the field, apart from
his and the dog's footprints, was virginal.

The police were called. Forensic examination established that
death had occurred some 10 hours before and was due to
exposure: the field had been snow-covered for more than two days.
The police were soon satisfied that the death had been accidental.

Explain.

HOMICIDE

Peter Collins stood accused of murder in the first degree. He pleaded self-defence, claiming he had been attacked by the victim with a kitchen knife. Evidence, one way or the other, was purely circumstantial and so, after some hectic plea-bargaining, a guilty plea of manslaughter was accepted and Collins was sentenced from three to seven years.

In prison, Collins found himself sharing a cell with a contract killer working for the Mafia, who had got away with a two-year sentence for possession of an offensive weapon, a handgun, without a licence.

A few months later, when the two men had become friendly, Collins confessed to his cellmate that he had got away with manslaughter but had in fact committed the murder at the request of a crime syndicate. With an air of professional pride, his cellmate, in turn, told Peter in detail about his own several contract killings. Perhaps Peter's syndicate might use the Mafia man's services too when he was released?

Some time later Peter Collins was transferred to another prison. Then a petition by his lawyer to the governor of the state was granted and Collins was released from prison, having served only five months of his sentence.

Explain how.

THE MONEY CHANGERS

After taking all necessary precautions, they agreed to meet in an old, disused warehouse. There were three tough-looking men in each group and bulges in their jackets betrayed the fact that all six were heavily armed. When the second group arrived, the leader of the first group opened a briefcase containing one hundred £50 notes.

To avoid any misunderstanding, it has to be stated that these banknotes were genuine, not numbered in sequence, and in pristine condition.

After a brief inspection, a member of the second group opened an envelope and paid £2,000 for the briefcase containing £5,000. Both parties seemed satisfied with the deal.

Explain.

THE JAMES DEAN
APPRECIATION
SOCIETY

The New York chapter of the James Dean Appreciation Society
is gathered for the screening of a new Hollywood docudrama
based on the life of its members' idol. Just as the movie reaches
the point of Dean's untimely death, the audience breaks out into
hysterical laughter and applause.

Why?

THE LOVERS

Pamela Wells was certainly no shrinking violet; just the opposite. She had three boyfriends on the go at the same time. The whole town, with the exception of the three men, seemed to know what was going on.

Early one morning, as he gazed at the gentle autumn rain through his office window, Inspector Jones received a call. It was a very distressed Paul Johnson, one of Pamela's boyfriends. He had arrived at her house, an isolated place on the outskirts of town, to find the front door ajar. On entering he had discovered her body; she had been bludgeoned to death. Inspector Jones told Paul to stay at the house, and he and his assistant left immediately for the scene of the crime.

Later that same day, after making extensive enquiries, Inspector Jones assembled his three main suspects, Paul Johnson and the other two boyfriends, Peter Smith and David Brown, at the station to make statements. Peter Smith stated that he had been out of town the previous evening. He had telephoned Pamela at 11 p.m. from his hotel and made arrangements to meet over the weekend. David Brown said that he had been at an office party, gotten quite drunk and spent the night at a colleague's house. Finally, Paul Johnson pointed out that he had seen Pamela the previous evening. They had had dinner and discussed a planned excursion the following day. He had left at about 9.30 p.m. and returned to his apartment on the other side of town.

Inspector Jones stared hard at Paul, then said: "Mr. Johnson, you are obviously lying about your whereabouts over the last twenty-four hours and I arrest you for the murder of Pamela Wells."

How did he know?

EYEWITNESS

Claire Vermont, the wealthy widow of the late Raymond Vermont, former publisher of mystery novels, owned a beautiful estate in Westchester. Late one evening she looked through the bay windows of her drawing room and to her horror saw a man strangling a woman.

Claire's first impulse was to open the door and attempt to stop the aggressor. However, she did not. She also did not phone the police although the telephone was in working order. In spite of the fact that she was not physically constrained in any way, she felt utterly helpless to intervene. She did not even call out for assistance to the live-in butler, although he was in the house.

Explain her strange behaviour.

THE VACANCY

Frank Kolmin was president of United Technologies, a multi-national company with offices spanning the globe. The head quarters, in New York's Empire State Building, occupied floors 12 through 15, but Frank was a roving ambassador for the group, regularly visiting South America, Europe and the Far East.

One day he placed the following advertizement in the *Wall Street Journal*:

"Part-time sales rep required for occasional overseas travel. No previous experience necessary, but working knowledge of French and Urdu are a condition. Excellent salary and commission. Suitable candidates may write, enclosing CV, to *Wall Street Journal*, Box #82."

Kolmin had no need for an applicant fitting that description. Why, then, did he advertize?

THE ICE-CREAM VENDOR

The 25th of July was the hottest day in living memory. On Brighton beach the ice-cream vendor did a roaring business, with a queue 10 yards long. When at long last it was 10-year-old Hassan's turn, the vendor looked at him and said, "I'm not selling ice cream to Arabs."

Hassan broke down in tears and ran to his father, Ali, who was fishing from the pier. When Ali heard the story, his face turned purple and he rushed to the ice-cream stand. "This is illegal race discrimination," he shouted, "and I will report you to the Race Relations Board."

The vendor remained unrepentant. "Sorry, I'm not selling to Arabs, but I will tell you something." He whispered a few words to Ali, whose angry face turned into a smile. He took Hassan by the hand and walked down the sea front to another ice-cream stall.

Can you explain this strange behaviour?

26

THE INTERCOM

Harry Thompson, managing director of Intertrust, decided that the time had come to introduce an intercom network into the office. True, they had a staff of only nine, but you had to move with the times. They next step would be to computerize the accounts and stock records in the hope that expansion of their printing business would justify the increased overheads. Thompson decided on an IBM system, with one master and eight substations.

One day a customer dropped in without prior appointment and insisted on seeing the boss. Thompson was very busy preparing a quotation for a big potential order but business is business and he decided to receive his visitor. All the fellow needed was some stationery. Not only did he haggle about the price but he engaged in an endless tirade on the shortcomings of the government's economic strategy. Thompson grew increasingly restless and, on the pretext of consulting his letterhead expert, Richard Booth, left the room and sent Richard in to take the brunt.

After more than half an hour Thompson had had enough. He went to the nearest intercom and called his office. "Get rid of that bore, he is just wasting our time," he told Richard, who did not answer; but the visitor left shortly thereafter. The order for letterheads never materialized and in fact Intertrust lost the customer for good.

Why?

THE SLIMMING PILL

After 10 years of intensive research, Dr Wertheimer of Johns Hopkins developed a slimming pill which was safe, had no side-effects and did not involve dieting of any sort. He demonstrated the effectiveness of the pill with a test group of 40 volunteers who took a pill twice daily, after lunch and dinner, for a period of five weeks.

When the results were logged, it transpired that the average weight loss of 10 pounds enjoyed by some participants in the test was almost precisely balanced by a weight gain suffered by the rest of the group.

Why?

28

LOST LUGGAGE

Alan Goide was proud of his Hartmann luggage, which he had bought at Harrods. He always travelled with a full set and although he had crossed the Atlantic more than 20 times during the last 12 months, the luggage looked like new. Quality shows!

Alan had just arrived at the Park Lane Hotel, Central Park South, after a supersonic Concorde trip from London. After a quick shower he wanted to unpack when he noticed that the combination would not open the lock on the largest case. He was just about to try and find a locksmith when he received a telephone call:

"Mr Goide, I'm glad I've found you. I was a co-passenger on Concorde and I have one of your Hartmann cases, while I presume you have one of mine. Can I come along to exchange?"

Alan Goide was relieved, and soon thereafter a hotel bell-boy brought up his suitcase, trading it for the other. He was slightly amused as the same mistake had happened to him before and was bound to occur to many Hartmann owners. Later, over a relaxing drink in the bar, he pondered how quickly the other passenger had been able to contact him. Probably through British Airways, he mused, when suddenly a thought struck him which made him contact the police.

What came into his mind?

THE STEELWORKER

David Edwin, 45 years old, lives in a high-rise apartment building within walking distance of the local steelworks, where he is employed as plant supervizor.

Every morning at 8 a.m. he walks down a flight of stairs and when he arrives at his destination he makes himself a cup of tea. He then reads the morning paper, which he has picked up from the news-vendor at the corner. Halfway through the paper, his eyelids get heavy and he falls asleep for a solid eight hours. Nonetheless, at the end of the month he looks forward to a nice productivity-linked bonus.

How does David get away with it?

THE INVENTION

He was known as Ollie though nobody knew, or for that matter cared, whether it was his first or last name. Ollie was a professional inventor. Come to him with a problem and he would design a suitable gadget to solve it.

One day he was approached with a rather unusual request. His customer needed a telephone and loudspeaker system which would receive calls, store them in a memory and resend them through the loudspeaker system after an interval of precisely five minutes, the set to be operated by remote control. If not switched on, the system would work like a standard telephone connection.

Unusual but not very difficult, Ollie thought, and using microchips the system was designed within a few hours. The £500 he received as a fee was considered "money for jam". Two months later he was arrested and accused of fraud, though eventually he would clear his name.

Explain the reason for his arrest.

THE FIFTY-DOLLAR FIND

A bank manager on his way home from work spotted a $50 banknote lying in the gutter. He picked it up, memorized the number to play in the lottery and happily pocketed it. When he got home, his wife happened to mention that the butcher's bill had arrived and came to exactly $50. With a grin, he produced the found money and she paid the butcher the following day. In turn, the butcher used the $50 banknote to pay the farmer from whom he bought his meat. The farmer then used it to pay his local merchant, who used it to pay his cleaning lady. The cleaning lady used the note to pay her overdraft at the bank.

As it happened, the cleaning lady deposited the banknote at the selfsame bank managed by the man who found it in the first place. Having remembered the number, he now discovered that it was counterfeit!

What was lost, if anything, in the whole transaction and by whom?

32

THE HIJACK

Shortly after 11 a.m. one October morning, two men were busy
unloading a shipment of dresses in Manhattan's garment district.
Just as they opened the back door of their delivery truck, three men
approached them, one brandishing an Uzi submachine gun, forced
them back into the truck, handcuffed, and locked them in.

No one passing by noticed the incident to report it to the police,
nor did the police have any prior information of the planned
hijack. Nevertheless, two 5th Precinct officers were on the lookout
for the truck as it approached the entrance to the Manhattan
Bridge and after spotting it they took up a pursuit that ended when
the raiders crashed in Brooklyn. Assuming that the police had no
other reason to stop or pursue the vehicle, how do you account for
their remarkable success in apprehending the hijackers?

THE BEACH

The scene: a deserted beach on a Pacific island. On the shoreline lies an upturned boat with a man lying alongside, attached to it by chains. The man has minor lacerations but is alive.

How did he get there?

WHAT ARE THEY?

"How much will one cost?" asked the customer in a hardware store. "Twenty cents," replied the clerk. "And how much will 12 cost?" "Forty cents." "Okay. I'll take 112." "Fine. That will be 60 cents."

What was the customer buying?

THE BURGLARS

John lives with his parents in a large flat in north London. One afternoon, while his parents were out, John was sitting on the sofa with Sophie, the neighbours' daughter, watching television. After a short while, Sophie left to buy some cigarettes. Suddenly two men burst into the flat and, ignoring John, proceeded to take the television set, a tape recorder and a personal computer, and then disappeared.

John had never seen either of the men before, nor was there any legal reason for them to remove the equipment, yet he remained sitting on the sofa throughout the incident without taking any action.

Explain.

36

TWO-FINGER SALUTE

This is a difficult one and will require clever questioning.

In medieval France, when two opposing forces joined battle it was the custom that the warriors lifted their right arm in a gesture of defiance, forming a "V" with two fingers. This sign was neither meant as abuse nor was it the Victory sign popularized by Winston Churchill during the Second World War.

What then did it signify?

37

THE PUNCTURES

A train was leaving Paris for the southern coast at the same time as a 200SL Mercedes. The driver of the Mercedes was unaware that both of the front tyres had slow punctures, and by the time the car arrived in Lyon those tyres were already completely flat. Although the driver did not change or have the tyres repaired, the Mercedes reached the French coast at the same time as the train.

Explain.

THE ORCHARD

Bob Wilson was very partial to fresh fruit and therefore had his own little orchard so that he could pick whatever fruit he desired straight from the tree. Cherries, apples, apricots… he had them all, and more.

One afternoon he fancied a few cherries, but as he was picking them he fell and although he was not climbing the tree, Bob was killed almost instantly from multiple fractures.

Explain.

THE CEMETERY

In the early post-war period – Vienna – the capital of Austria – had
run out of space for additional cemeteries. The Allied bombing
and the advancing Red Army had increased the demand for burial
space, and the local administration established by the occupying
powers tried to find a solution. Several choices were considered.
Legislating for compulsory cremation was voted down. Replacing
existing graves over 100 years old caused a storm of indignation
from the Church and the descendants.

Finally one member came up with a bright idea. Can you do so
as well?

FOREIGN EXCHANGE

One of the break-away republics from the former Soviet Union needed new banknotes with a high denomination to cope with inflation. Their newly-formed central bank approached a British company specializing in the printing of banknotes for foreign governments. After some haggling about the cost, a purchase order was issued and an artist's drawing of the design sent by special courier to the London printer.

The printers, using advanced photographic technology, produced two sets of master plates and printed one million banknotes under the customary strict-security measures. When the print-run was completed, they dispatched one set of master plates, the notes and an invoice to their customer.

A few days later, the printer in London received a strongly-worded fax from the customer, refusing to pay and threatening litigation as the banknotes received were completely useless. The new notes were obviously an exact replica of the artist's drawing and the paper used was in accordance with specifications. What went wrong?

After considering the fax for a little while, the printer, who was a member of Mensa with an IQ of 161, sent a fax in reply, whereupon he was visited by the country's ambassador, who first apologized and then thanked him profusely. He handed the printer a banker's draft for the full amount of the invoice plus a bonus of 50 per cent.

Can you explain this extraordinary turn-about?

POOLS OF WATER

A strange but short-lived phenomenon baffled employees of pubs and clubs in Camden, north London. Pools of water appeared under the cigarette-vending machines.

What do you think had happened?

THE HUNDRED-DOLLAR NOTE

Steve was picked up by the police in the drugstore as he was about to pay for his purchase with a hundred-dollar note. Three thousand dollars were found on him, all in $100 bills. He was indicted in connection with the banknotes and for no other crime or felony.

Although it was found that the bills were genuine, not counterfeit, and that Steve could also prove that the money was not stolen or obtained illegally in any way, he received a two-year suspended prison term.

Why?

43

CELL PHONE

Wolfgang Reinisch was returning to London from a bridge tournament in Las Vegas. As always he was travelling first class with British Airways.

Just as they touched down at Heathrow, Wolfgang noticed that his cell phone, an expensive piece of equipment, had disappeared; another first-class passenger must have taken it while he was asleep. The plane was now taxiing and would arrive at the disembarking point in a few minutes, and once passengers had dispersed there was no hope of recovering it. Fortunately Wolfgang was sitting next to the famous Belgian detective, Monsieur Hercule Poirot. Poirot contemplated for a brief moment and then made a suggestion which recovered the phone within a few minutes.

What did Poirot suggest?

HIT-AND-RUN

One late winter evening, Frank Rosetti was caught speeding on the M4 in his BMW. After his driving licence and insurance certificate had been checked, he was asked to submit to a breathalyzer test, to which he readily agreed. This proved to be entirely negative. In fact the alcohol content in his blood was practically zero, and therefore he was let off with a caution.

A little farther up the M4 the same BMW was involved in a hit-and-run accident. The victim remembered the registration number and Frank was arrested the next morning. He denied having driven the BMW and in fact had reported the car stolen at about 10 p.m. This was hardly conclusive as the accident had taken place at 8.30 p.m. and the police officer who had stopped Rosetti for speeding at precisely 8.10 p.m. positively identified him.

In court Frank's lawyer pleaded that it was not safe to rely on the officer's identification as he saw the driver only in darkness. to clinch the issue in favour of the defence he produced three witnesses who testified that Frank Rosetti, who was a taster for Elite Wines Ltd, had tasted a range of wines all afternoon and the zero breathalyzer result proved conclusively that the accused could not have been the driver.

Did the defence succeed?

LOST

Eight-year-old Bobby, obviously lost, was running down Baker Street looking frantically left and right for John. People looked at him sympathetically but no one offered to help. Suddenly he stopped dead in his tracks as he heard a familiar noise, although nobody else in the street seemed to hear it. Immediately he turned round and ran excitedly in the direction he had originally come from. Soon he was reunited with John.

Explain.

OVER THE
LIMIT

With the festive season approaching, the chief of police ordered
a clamp-down on drinking and driving. In line with the order,
two of his officers were keeping a discreet watch on an exclusive
downtown club when they saw a customer stagger out of the door
and fall down on the snow-covered ground. After a few seconds he
picked himself up, stumbled to his car and fumbled for the keys.
Eventually he got the door open and managed to start the car,
grinding the gears before moving off in a zigzag course.

The police followed in their car, stopped him and he was given
a breathalyzer test. The test was negative. Obviously something
was wrong with the equipment, as the man reeked of alcohol.
The officers took him to the police station for another test. Again
negative. A blood test showed the same result. The police were
baffled.

Can you solve the mystery?

THE PEARL NECKLACE

Caroline was a salaried companion to Margaret Stenton, the wealthy widow of a media tycoon.

One day, window-shopping on 5th Avenue, Mrs Stenton saw a beautiful pearl necklace in Harry Winston's window. She decided that she had to have it. They asked for Winston, an old friend of the family, who had the necklace brought in. The pearls were of an exquisite pink hue and Caroline thought it was the most beautiful piece of jewellery she had ever seen. Harry Winston assured Margaret the pearls were not cultured but those for which pearl divers in the Bay of Bengal spend their lives looking.

One weekend when Margaret Stenton was out of town, Caroline was invited to a ball by her fiancé. She borrowed one of Margaret's gowns, for which she had permission, and also took the pearl necklace from the safe, for which she had no permission.

In the underground car park of the hotel where the ball was being held she was mugged and robbed of the necklace and her handbag. Caroline was devastated. Her first impulse was to contact the police and confess to Mrs Stenton that she had taken the necklace from the safe without permission. She quickly changed her mind. The necklace was not insured and if she had told the police and Mrs Stenton, they might have suspected a conspiracy and that she had arranged the mugging herself. Caroline was now in a state of utter panic.

She immediately contacted Harry Winston and asked him
if he could supply a replacement identical to the original.
He confirmed that he could do this but it would cost a small
fortune. Caroline withdrew all her savings and borrowed the
rest from her fiancé and friends. She collected the replacement
necklace, which she promptly put back in the safe.

This unfortunate incident completely wrecked Caroline's life. In
spite of extreme economy she was unable to repay the loan on time.
Her friends deserted her and her fiancé broke off the engagement.

A few years later Mrs Stenton was due to attend a function and
invited Caroline to accompany her. She then uttered one sentence to
her employee, which made her go white and break down in floods
of tears.

What did she say?

CIRCUMSTANTIAL EVIDENCE

Fred and Rona Miller seemed a devoted couple. He was the manager of the local post office and Rona assisted in running a kindergarten.

One morning, without prior notice, Rona failed to turn up to work. Fred did not seem to know where Rona was. Days went by, and Rona's mysterious disappearance started tongues wagging.

A week later Fred produced a letter he had just received, purporting to be from Rona, and showed it to an inquisitive neighbour. In a nutshell, the letter asked Fred's forgiveness but explained that she had decided to start a new life somewhere else before it was too late.

It was not long before the police took an interest in the case. The letter was considered by an expert to be a forgery when compared with samples of Rona's handwriting. Forensic examination of Fred's car found traces of blood which were not of his blood group. The most suspicious clue was found in Rona's dressing room. She had left most of her clothes and jewellery behind.

Fred was duly arraigned and although no body was found, the circumstantial evidence was overwhelming. He was found guilty of murder and sentenced to 15 years in prison.

A year later new evidence emerged in Fred's favour which was so conclusive that he was immediately released, only to be re-arrested and accused of conspiracy to defraud. Explain.

THE BLACK BOX

A man is seen in an apartment, going from room to room. Each time he holds a small metal object to the floor and the walls.

What is he up to?

THE PILOT

Ara Oztemel was a senior pilot for Delta Airlines' 747 fleet. One morning he took off as scheduled at 07.45 in spite of an unfavourable weather report; it is international practice that in case of doubtful weather conditions a captain can use his own discretion.

True enough, the weather deteriorated suddenly and the aircraft crashed after 30 minutes. Fortunately nobody was seriously hurt and while the plane suffered extensive damage, Delta Airlines took no action whatsoever.

Explain.

THE
EXPLORERS

Two field workers were sent from a base to explore a mineral
find in a remote area. They were about to collect samples when
they were attacked by vicious animals. Immediately they stopped
working to return to the safety of their home base. One of the
explorers withdrew extremely slowly, keeping a watchful eye
on the animals. The other panicked and fled at great speed.
Although the panicked explorer escaped being attacked, he died
as soon as he reached the base, while his colleague survived.

Explain.

52

THE SERIAL KILLER

Andrew Scott, the serial killer, was finally apprehended by Federal Agent Connolly near Reno, at the foothills of the Sierra Nevada.

Connolly was ordered to fly him over the mountain range to San Francisco to be arraigned. The only plane available was a Lockheed monoplane trainer, just big enough to accommodate the pilot and the killer handcuffed to Connolly.

Half an hour after take-off the plan crashed in a devastating snow storm. The pilot died on impact but the two passengers survived with leg injuries: the accident and the storm had caused their few belongings, including some of their clothes, to be strewn over a wide area.

When the rescue team arrived Connolly told them to hand him the gun and the key to the handcuffs. Scott countered by saying that he was the law enforcement officer and Connolly was a dangerous criminal, and therefore the gun and keys should be handed to him.

The items were eventually found, but the rescuers had to decide whom to believe. No identification papers could be found and to transport the men handcuffed to each other was impossible. Radio contact with the outside had been lost and there seemed to be no way to establish their identities. Finally Connolly whispered something in the team leader's ear, which decided the issue.

What was it?

D-DAY

Just before the Normandy landings sex shops in Britain were doing a roaring business. This unexpected bonanza had nothing to do with the libido of the Allied Forces on British soil, however.

What then was the reason for the increased turnover?

THE PHONE RINGS

Eight men were sitting around the boardroom table and one man, armed with a sub-machine gun, stood at the door. Everyone was silent and the atmosphere became tense. Suddenly the telephone rang. At that moment one of the men jumped up and took a header through the window.

Can you find an explanation?

55

DAY OUT

The social club in Southville had saved for the whole year to finance an outing to the country fair in Northville, about half an hour away.

On a bright Sunday morning they set out in high spirits, looking forward to an enjoyable day at the fair. Ten minutes later Mr and Mrs Jones, prominent members of the club, turned round and headed back toward Southville. Yet after a further 20 minutes the couple, together with the other club members, arrived at their destination. They did not use any speedier transport to catch up with their friends.

How did they do it?

56

PLACE OF WORK

Norman Selway has spent five straight days and nights at his place of work. Even though there is nothing for him to do there, he was not asked by his employer to stay, and he has a perfectly happy home life. Further, during the last two days he has not eaten or taken a drink, although there is food and water just a few feet away. There are also several restaurants so close that he can see them from where he sits.

Three days ago, his wife rang to tell him that he had won the city lottery and although they need the money urgently, Norman has done nothing about claiming his prize. The day before, his only son was presented with the Congressional Medal of Honour but John did not attend.

Norman is not sick or suffering from agoraphobia, and he does not have any other physical disability. He can move about freely and he is neither crazy nor on hunger strike. Also he is not taking part in any experiment, or trying to win a bet or get his name into the *Guinness Book of Records*. He is completely alone and, oh yes, he has a desk job too.

What is happening?

DUSK OR DAWN?

Norman Bronstein, a sports enthusiast and loner, would try anything that presented a physical challenge of endurance and danger. On this occasion, white-water rafting in the Amazon, he set off alone from Manaus one winter morning. At first all went well, but early in the afternoon his raft entered some rapids and struck a rock; Norman was thrown clear onto the shore. His raft and all belongings, including his pocket watch, were lost. He lay for days, unconscious from a head wound. When he finally came to, it was twilight. Although dazed, Norman realized that it was dusk and that he would have to spend another night before he could be rescued. How did he know instantly that it was dusk, not dawn?

THE RUNNER

The crowd in the stadium were on their feet, cheering and clapping. It was the end of the 10,000 metres race in the world championships. Jonathan Cansino was leading the field and looked certain to take the medal. He was 3 metres from the finish when the runner from Nigeria passed him and crossed the line. Jonathan glanced across in horror, which quickly turned to jubilation, and threw his arms up in triumph.

What had happened?

THE
HELICOPTER

This is a true story. There used to be a helicopter service operated by Pan American World Airways from mid-town Manhattan on the East River to Kennedy Airport, and return.

One evening it was raining heavily. I checked in to fly to JFK. The baggage handlers were loading the luggage while the passengers waited under cover until called. The helicopter engine had just started when I noticed that one of my suitcases had been left behind. I got hold of it and rushed out into the rain to hand it to the handlers before they closed the hatch. Two of the airline employees jumped me in a tackle and threw me to the ground when I had almost reached the helicopter.

Instead of apologizing, they brusquely ordered me back to the waiting area.

Explain.

60

THE KEYS

Andrew Taylor, a fairly successful author of mysteries and thrillers, left his house in Cambridge at 8 a.m. to travel to London to see Raymond Berstein, the managing editor of his publishing company, who had expressed his dissatisfaction with the ending of Andrew's latest book.

Andrew had decided that he would go on to Bristol after the meeting to see his ex-wife, with whom he was still on excellent terms, and his two children. He was also looking forward to a couple of days of relaxation.

His meeting with Raymond went very well and together they agreed on changes to the ending of the book, which improved it tremendously. After his trip to Bristol, Andrew would return to Cambridge refreshed to do the necessary rewrites.

As Andrew was travelling by train to Bristol he suddenly realized that he didn't have his house keys with him. On arrival he telephoned Raymond and asked him if he had left his keys in his office. "No problem, Andrew old boy, they were on my desk so I have already put them in the mail to you."

Andrew exploded with rage. "You idiot," he said angrily, "how could you do such a stupid thing." Raymond was very hurt by this outburst and could not understand why Andrew was so mad.

Can you?

61

THE SAWMILL

Boris Kerensky was plant supervizor of the largest sawmill in Novgorod, an industrial centre in the northern regions of the Soviet Union.

One evening at the end of the day-shift, Ivan saw his friend Boris leaving the sawmill with a wheelbarrow full of wood shavings. Ivan was the guard at the factory gate whose duty was to ensure that nothing was smuggled out of the factory to be sold on the black market. Small tools were in particular demand, fetching high prices. Ivan examined the load of wood shavings conscientiously, but found nothing and let Boris pass.

Next day the same thing happened and again Ivan found nothing. After several repeat performances Ivan could no longer contain his curiosity! "Come on, Boris, you can't tell me that all you are doing is helping to get rid of the rubbish, there must be a method in your madness." After some hesitation Boris confided in Ivan, but not before he had sworn his friend to secrecy.

What was Boris after?

DANGER IN
THE AIR

Following the sudden disappearance of a passenger, two airline
stewardesses – upset as a result of the incident – began to quarrel.
Soon one of them, very distraught, became so agitated that she
totally lost control. Running to the door of the plane, she opened
it and jumped. She had no parachute (they are not provided on
civilian flights); nevertheless, she survived with only a sprained ankle.

Was she just incredibly lucky?

THE CRIME

In some states in the United States a certain crime is punishable, and those who attempt it are usually indicted. However, any perpetrator who is successful is never prosecuted.

What is the crime?

64

THE MAQUIS

During the Second World War the French underground, called the Maquis, was organised soon after the fall of Paris. They were actively supported by the French government in exile and by the British Secret Service.

The Gestapo tried to infiltrate the organization, but vetting procedures adopted by the underground cells were rigorous and exceedingly effective. On several occasions such undercover agents were discovered and subsequently shot.

The cells met frequently in safe houses to plan subversive operations. During one such meeting a different agenda was tabled. Jean-Claude, code named "Le Loup", a prominent member of the cell present, was subjected to severe interrogation. He was accused of collaboration with the enemy. Finally, a photograph was introduced showing Jean-Claude entering Gestapo headquarters.

Le Loup broke down and offered no excuses, whereupon René, the leader of the cell, produced a gun and ordered Georges, who had only recently joined, to shoot the traitor. Georges, who had never killed a man before, hesitated only a split second and, being a fervent patriot, obeyed the command.

However René knew that Jean-Claude was a loyal member of the Maquis, innocent of any betrayal. Why, then, did he give the order?

65

THE JUDGEMENT

A man stood before the judge, charged with killing a long-eared owl, a protected species. Pleading guilty but with extenuating circumstances, the man explained that he had been on a camping trip with his family in a remote region. One day, while they were all swimming in a nearby lake, their camp caught fire and was completely destroyed, leaving them without shelter or food. After going hungry for two days, they came upon the bird, and the man threw a rock that succeeded in killing it. It was cooking and eating the owl, he allowed, that helped them to survive.

The judge, after hearing his story, decided to let the man off. As the man was about to leave the court, the judge called out, "Just as a matter of interest, what does a long-eared owl taste like?" The man paused, thought for a moment and then answered the judge's question.

The judge then called him back. "On second thoughts, I retract my earlier decision," he said. "You will pay a fine of $2,000, and consider yourself lucky I do not send you to prison." What did the man say to cause the judge to reverse his original decision?

THE OPERATION

A man went to the hospital with a suspected malignant tumour in his left kidney. Several tests were made but the results were all negative. Nevertheless, the man insisted on an operation to remove the kidney.

Why?

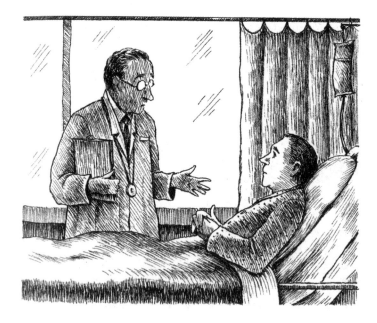

67

THE CONTRACT

Stephen was about to leave the country but wanted to hand some important documents personally on his way to the airport to his partner Dave. When he phoned, Stephen got Dave's answering machine, but knowing that Dave was in the habit of checking for messages at regular intervals he said, "Dave, this is important! I have the Duplex Corporation contract which must be exchanged this afternoon. Please meet me without fail in exactly 40 minutes at the corner of 5th Avenue and 55th Street. I can only wait for five minutes, but it's all I need to hand you the papers and give you verbal instructions of a highly confidential nature. Thank you." At that moment the limousine arrived to take Stephen to JFK airport.

The car arrived at the designated corner with three minutes to spare. Stephen had the car wait, confident that Dave would arrive at any moment. After 10 minutes, when Dave did not turn up, Stephen was forced to continue to the airport even though an important deal was in jeopardy. Why did Dave, who had, incidentally, heard the message in good time and was not physically prevented, not meet his partner?

TABLE MANNERS

I was very flattered to receive an invitation to the Lord Mayor's gala dinner at the Savoy: I am just a humble photographer, though I suspect that the society photographs and column I am doing for the *Sunday News* had something to do with it.

I had to hire tails from Moss Bros for this occasion, and as the sleeves and trousers were inches too long I felt like a cotton-picker dressed for a fancy-dress party. The food was only so-so, and there was nothing interesting to report except for an incident which baffled me until I asked the maitre d' for an explanation.

Lady Jane Smith-Corona was sitting at the next table chatting amiably with her husband, Sir Archibald, when the soup was served. Lady Jane tasted one spoonful and stopped. She continued to stir listlessly with her spoon and then whispered something to her husband. Sir Archibald inspected the soup without tasting it and called the head waiter. After a brief *sotto voce* conversation, the maitre d' produced a straw, with which Lady Jane finished her soup while all the other guests continued to use the more conventional implement – a spoon.

Can you explain her strange table manners?

69

THE ASSASSIN

When Tessino, the Consigliori to the Vito Bracci family, was found shot dead in his car, no one was surprised. It was an open secret that Tessino had skimmed the profits from the Ritz Casino when he was temporarily in charge of one of the most profitable ventures in the Bracci empire; it was equally certain that Vito Bracci or one of his henchmen was responsible. But suspecting or even knowing, and proving, are two different things.

The facts surrounding the crime were quite unusual. Tessino was killed by three shots, one of which demolished his expensive wristwatch, so that the time of the shooting, 7.34 p.m., could be accurately established. At that time the area surrounding Tessino's limousine was crowded, yet nobody appeared to have heard the shots or noticed the murder.

Can you think of an explanation?

THE BIRTHDAY
PARTY

Joan's three-year marriage to Albert had been tempestuous. Periods of happiness were cruelly interrupted by vicious quarrels, for no particular reason that Joan could think of. On one occasion Albert had even hit her, though he had immediately apologized and asked her to forgive him. It was clearly a love-hate relationship, but unfortunately the hate periods became progressively more frequent.

On one occasion, when Albert started to throw things, Joan had confided in her twin sister, Catherine. Catherine had promised to talk to Albert and to impress on him that by his unreasonable conduct he was jeopardizing his marriage. It seemed to have the desired effect: Albert appeared to be a changed man.

On the day before Joan's 25th birthday she came home unexpectedly and found Albert sitting at his desk, writing. He seemed embarrassed and Joan became suspicious. Later that day she went through his desk. One drawer was locked, but Joan had no problem in finding a key to fit. Under some papers she found a jewellery box containing a beautiful bracelet with a handwritten note:

> "My dearest, for your 25th birthday, accept this gift
> as a token of my undying love and affection.
>
> Albert."

At that moment Joan was overcome with intense happiness and ready to forgive Albert for all the heartache he had caused her so often. Not to spoil the surprize she put the box back where she had found it.

Next evening at the birthday party, when all the guests had arrived, Catherine helped her to open the presents. When she came to Albert's birthday gift she seemed at first surprized, then burst into tears and left the party.

Why?

THE CLAQUERS

Theatre directors in pre-war Vienna used to employ the services of young people, mostly students, to attend performances and demonstrate by repeated and enthusiastic hand-clapping and other gestures that the play was an undoubted success. Paid clappers in French are called *les claques*, hence the name. In addition to free entry, the claquers also receive a modest payment at the end of the performance.

One evening a French farçe by Feydeau was on the programme and the manager selected 12 young men from around 30 who had queued for the job. They waited for about 10 minutes after curtain-up before starting their work. At first it was subdued laughter and clapping at every opportune moment. Then two of them, hoping for a bonus, shouted: "Funny, funny, funny," and finished off with a prolonged belly laugh. The audience did not apparently share the mirth of the claquers. In fact hissing noises were heard from time to time. The team ended their assignment with a roar of laughter and wild clapping just before curtain-down.

After the performance and back at the office to collect their bonus they found instead an irate theatre director who refused to pay and a contrite manager who had been dismissed.

Why?

AVOIDING THE TRAIN

A man was walking along a railway track when he spotted an express train speeding toward him. To avoid it, he jumped off the track, but before he jumped he ran 10 feet toward the train.

Why?

IN THE PARK

It was a warm, sunny day and Jane decided to take 3-year-old Sally to the park. When they arrived, Jane spread a towel on the ground and watched as Sally played in the grass nearby. Suddenly a large Rottweiler charged across the field straight toward Sally. Instead of panicking, Jane just watched, apparently unconcerned.

Why?

THE SPY

During the First World War, a German spy succeeded in obtaining a copy of a map showing the location of Allied mines in the North Sea and the Atlantic.

The German Navy was satisfied that the information was correct, as only a short time before two of their ships had been blown up by mines shown on the map. The spy had obtained access to the document, which was marked "Top Secret", by befriending a secretary working in the Admiralty. Although the circumstances were known to British counter-intelligence, the secretary was not arrested.

Why?

PIT BULL TERRIER

Tom the butcher was trying to deliver a leg of lamb and some sausages to the cottage of Jack the cobbler. However, there was nobody at home. Somewhat annoyed, Tom was about to turn back when a gust of wind blew his new hat toward Jack's cherry tree. Trying to retrieve it, Tom faced a slight problem. Tied to the tree on a long leash was Kim, the pit bull terrier well-known and feared for his viciousness, and the hat was just within his reach.

How could Tom recover his hat without being attacked by Kim?

DEATH IN THE CAR

A man was shot to death while in his car. There were no powder marks on his clothing, which indicated that the gunman was outside the car. However, all the windows were closed and the doors locked. After a closer inspection was made, the only bullet-holes discovered were on the man's body.

How was he murdered?

THE OPERATION

A Canadian nuclear scientist was operated on for a brain tumour on 26 July last year. The operation was unsuccessful and the scientist was cremated on 25 July in the same year.

How is this possible?

THE KIDNAP

The first ransom demand was made by telephone two days after Eric Watson's disappearance: the kidnappers wanted $3 million in used notes. This was far beyond the family's availability and over the next few days negotiations succeeded in reducing the ransom to $0.5 million dollars.

The police had been involved from the start and had advized the family to insist on tangible proof that Eric was still alive before parting with any money. The following day a photograph was found in the letter-box of Eric holding a copy of the *Sun* of the previous day.

Detective Inspector O'Reilly was a little sceptical: "This photograph could easily be a fake and needs to be examined by the police laboratory." Two hours later Dr Bernstein, head of the laboratory, handed the photo back to O'Reilly. "This is undoubtedly genuine," he said, "and I have even better news." He whispered something in O'Reilly's ear. The same afternoon the kidnappers' lair was raided and Eric Watson freed.

Explain.

THE HEIR

The king dies and two men, the true heir and an impostor, both claim to be his long-lost son. Both fit the description of the rightful heir: about the right age, height, colouring and general appearance. Finally, one of the elders proposes a test to identify the true heir. One man agreed to the test while the other flatly refused. The one who agreed was immediately sent on his way, and the one who refused correctly identified as the rightful heir.

Why?

ACCIDENT PRONE

Steve Jones, an architect, was inspecting his latest project, a brownstone conversion in the upper east side of Manhattan. He was very proud of the finished building and was inspecting the roof when he slipped and fell over the edge to the concrete forecourt below, landing catlike on all fours. Surprisingly he escaped with only heavy bruising and shock.

A week later he was feeling fit enough to return to the building, and again finished up on the roof. In a stroke of amazing bad luck and in an almost complete replay of the previous week's events, he tripped and fell, again landing on all fours in the same spot on the concrete forecourt. This time, however, he broke both legs and arms, and was hospitalized for several weeks.

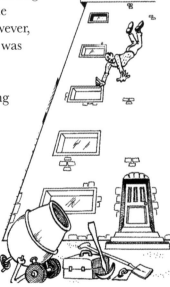

The amazing thing was that during his fall he realized that, for a reason beyond his control, on this occasion he would be badly injured. How did he know?

81

THE SUSPECT

Clifford Bradshaw, the banker, was found stabbed to death by his live-in housekeeper one Sunday morning. The prime suspect was his nephew Brian, who was Clifford's sole heir. According to the housekeeper, the two had often quarrelled, sometimes virulently, and yet were dependent on each other emotionally, having no other living relatives.

Brian was in the habit of visiting Clifford regularly after work, about 5 p.m. On the Saturday evening before Clifford's death, Brian had come for dinner and had left about 11 p.m. No fingerprints could be found on the knife except Clifford's. The housekeeper, who disliked Brian intensely, told the police that his nephew was the last person to see Clifford alive and obviously had a strong motive as Clifford had been considering changing his will in her favour. However, under close questioning the housekeeper had to admit that she had been in her room when Brian left and that she had heard the two arguing in the corridor as the clock chimed the hour. She had then heard Clifford's study door slam, and through the window she had seen Brian leave the house, step into his chauffeured limousine and be driven off.

The housekeeper also had to admit that it was impossible for Brian to have returned without her knowing. Furthermore, Brian had a foolproof alibi, having spent the rest of the night with friends playing poker. The post-mortem established the time of death that night at between 10.30 and 12.30.

In view of the circumstances, the housekeeper became the obvious suspect, although without the will change she did not seem to have had a motive. Suicide was a possibility, but unlikely. In fact, as was later established, Brian had committed the murder.

How?

When the housekeeper later went over her statement she suddenly realized the fatal flaw in Brian's plan.

What was it?

82

THE STAGECOACH ROBBERY

Billy the Kid was caught red-handed trying to hold up the Wells Fargo delivery from Denver to the San Francisco office. Dave, the sheriff, had sprung a trap acting on confidential information.

Billy was locked in a cell to await transport to San Francisco the next day. However, the Kid managed to escape on horseback with a head-start of a few hours. The sheriff's posse could have caught up with him, had they known in which direction he went. Then, by a stroke of luck, it began to snow. The posse fanned out, knowing they were likely to find Billy's tracks in the snow. Sure enough, they crossed them one hour later. It seemed that the Kid was heading for Phoenix. The horse's tracks indicated it was slightly lame, so that the posse was likely to shortly catch up with Billy.

After less than an hour, the track led them to a log cabin with stables attached. They could see Billy's footprints in the snow leading from the stables to the cabin. The Kid was trapped. The sheriff shouted two warnings, but there was no response. When the posse stormed the cabin it was empty; so were the stables.

Assuming there were no other tracks in the snow except the horse's to the stables and Billy's to the cabin, how could the culprit and his horse have dissolved into thin air?

83

THE TUNNEL

The train from Zurich was approaching Chur. The first-class compartment was occupied by Karl and Lisa Hohl (a Swiss couple from Lausanne), Bob (a Londoner with an RAF moustache), Heinz Klausner (a businessman from Hamburg), a beautiful young blonde from Paris and Greta (a girl student from Sweden). All of them were on their way to St Moritz, looking forward to a vacation in the sun and snow.

Klausner, in high spirits and slightly drunk, soon made a nuisance of himself. He started by poking fun at Bob's handle-bar moustache; he then made disparaging remarks about Swiss men and finally, fancying himself to be irresistible, turned his attention to the ladies. First he tried to snuggle up to Lisa, who was trying to sleep. He then put his arm around Greta, who was too shy to protest. At the same time he made suggestive remarks in atrocious French to the girl from Paris, who was trying to read *L'Express*.

Just then the train entered the last tunnel before Chur, plunging the compartment into total darkness. Suddenly there was a sound of a loud kiss followed by a punch. When the train emerged into broad daylight, consternation and tension pervaded the compartment. Karl Hohl looked angry, Lisa was fully awake, Greta was blushing, Bob seemed unconcerned and the girl from Paris held the magazine close to her eyes. Heinz Klausner sported a black eye and looked flabbergasted.

Can you guess what had happened?

84

THE LONER

John Miller, at 63, was a disgruntled man. He lived in a cheap rented apartment and had no relatives or friends, only a few nodding acquaintances from the bar around the corner. He had joined the US Mail at 18 and was still there, in the sorting office. Younger men were promoted over him, and John had the feeling that if he were to die tomorrow, nobody would notice, let alone miss him.

John decided that he had to do something spectacular before he faded away altogether. If he could not become famous, lacking any remarkable talent, perhaps he could become notorious. First only a pipe-dream, the idea of his name appearing in print took hold until it became an obsession.

He bought a gun from a dubious character and bided his time, waiting for the right opportunity. This came one Saturday afternoon, when he knew he would see the President on 5th Avenue. When the President appeared, John fired two shots at close range. The President collapsed, bleeding profusely from a shoulder wound. John was overpowered and arrested. He was questioned for three solid days and then released on nominal bail. When he appeared in court, he was found guilty and sentenced to 120 hours of community service.

Was the judge unduly lenient?

THE ACCIDENT

Tracy and Scott were holidaying in Florida. One morning they were driving in a hired car from Hallandale to Miami Beach. Tired from a night on the town, Scott fell asleep at the wheel and the car careered off the road and hit a lamp-post.

Scot suffered only a broken nose and a few scratches, but Tracy had more serious injuries and was hospitalised for three weeks. On recovery she sued Scott and was awarded $20,000 and $2,000 for medical bills. Although Scott – a student – could ill afford such a loss, he was pleased with the outcome.

Explain.

A SAFE PLACE

Leo Halpern leaves home. When he tries to return, a man wearing a mask blocks his path.

(a) What is Leo doing?
(b) What is the masked man's occupation?
(c) Where is Leo's "safe place"?

87

THE FANCY-DRESS BALL

Martin Hofmann was a foreign exchange dealer in the Zurich branch of Intertrust AG, a medium-sized private bank. Management decided to arrange a number of social events in addition to the annual Christmas party to promote the team spirit among staff. Martin received an invitation, signed by the manager, to one of these events: a fancy-dress ball at the Baur-Au-Lac, one of the most exclusive five-star hotels in town. The motto for the ball was "A night at the court of Louis XV".

Martin thought long and hard as to what to wear. In the end he hired the outfit of a court jester. When he entered the ballroom he created a minor sensation.

Assuming the date, time and venue were all correct, what did he do wrong?

88

THE SYSTEM

Two men, Frank and Johnny, were walking from the Hotel de Paris in Monte Carlo to the Winter Casino, just a few steps away. Frank, wearing his tuxedo, walked straight in while Johnny, in a plain dark suit, lingered outside for a few minutes before going into the Salle Privée. Johnny took a seat at the roulette table opposite Frank, but ignored him as if they were strangers, then both men started to gamble heavily, but only on *chances simples*. If Frank bet on red, Johnny bet the same amount on black. The same with pair and impair, and so on.

It so happened that another Hotel de Paris guest who knew them was watching the two gamblers. After a little while he turned to his wife: "Look what Frank and Johnny are doing – doesn't seem like much of a system. They can't win, but will lose every time zero comes up."

What do you think was going on?

THE NEWSPAPER

Although Lisa and Joan were reading the same newspaper copy at the same time, they could not see each other. It is obvious that there must have been sufficient light, and there could have been nothing wrong with their eyesight.

Why could they neither see nor touch each other?

90

VICTORIA STATION

Both Brian and Bill were going from Marble Arch to Victoria Station. Brian was driving at normal speed, while Bill started on foot. Traffic was light, and although Bill ran part of the way and Brian reached an average speed of 25 miles per hour, both arrived at Victoria Station at the same time. How was this possible?

91

DEVOTED
COUPLE

James and Catherine Barker were an extremely happy and
contented couple in their early sixties. Catherine had given
up her job to become a full-time housewife when she married
James, and he had only 12 months to go before he retired as
managing director of a successful engineering company.

James had always been an active man and his study was
crammed with trophies that he had won in various sporting
activities. He now took great pleasure in cleaning the trophies
once a week and Catherine was happy to let him get on with it.
Although James had recently appeared rather pale and tired, he
assured Catherine that everything was alright.

One Saturday evening, James had settled down in his study for
the trophy-polishing ritual, while Catherine watched the 6 p.m.
news in the parlour. As the broadcast was ending, Catherine
went to the study to ask James if he wanted a cup of tea. She
found the door locked and could hear her husband talking to
someone. Wondering how anyone could have arrived without
her knowing, she knocked on the door. Suddenly she heard her
husband cry out "Put down that knife!" and then came a scream.

Catherine became hysterical and ran out into the garden to
look through the study window. It was open and she could see
her husband slumped in his chair with a large knife embedded
in his chest. She ran screaming to her neighbours and they
immediately phoned for the police.

The homicide detectives were very quickly on the scene. James had been stabbed through the heart and died instantly. There were no fingerprints on the knife nor any sign of a scuffle or evidence that anything had been taken. The Chief Inspector looked at his colleague and said, "Where's the motive?" His colleague shook his head.

Well, what was the motive?

92

THE BIRTHDAY

Alice and George were window shopping in London's Bond Street. As they passed a jeweller, Alice stopped and admired a bracelet, one of three, with the motif of a leopard silhouetted in semi-precious stones. Reading her mind, her husband said, "Darling, I would love to make this your birthday present, but it must be far beyond my budget." "Let's ask, just for fun," ventured Alice, and they entered the store. As requested, the sales clerk fetched the leopard bracelet. Alice tried it on and looked pleadingly at her husband. Asked the price, the clerk hesitated for a brief moment and then said, "£250 for payment in cash." George could not hide his surprise, as the piece looked much more costly. "The stones are paste," volunteered the clerk by way of explanation and he offered to reserve the bracelet until George could return with the cash. At home, Alice waited impatiently for George and her new bracelet. When he arrived there was a smug smile on his face: "Darling, you won't believe this, but I showed the bracelet to Oscar, the jeweller in Swiss Cottage, and he offered me £800 for it. Now I can buy you all three bracelets!"

When Alice recovered from her shock at this turn of events, she was near tears. "No, George, I have changed my mind. I don't want a bracelet. In fact, I don't want any birthday present at all."

Explain.

93

THE
ARCHAEOLOGIST

Milos Sudsic enjoyed a world-wide reputation as a successful
archaeologist with many important finds to his credit. One of his
lesser-known exploits is the subject of the following story.

Recently Milos travelled to Greece accompanied by two assistants.
He contacted the governor of the famous monastic community
of Mount Athos to negotiate a 12-month excavation lease of a
well-defined three-acre site on the north side of the mountain.
The lease terms were agreed at £100,000, giving Milos the right
to excavate for 12 months and to keep any finds on condition
that these items were all listed. Three guards were assigned to
supervize the excavations to ensure that Milos limited himself to
the designated area.

Already on the third day Milos and his crew struck pay dirt.
One of the guards, his curiosity aroused by excited shouts,
approached the site. What he saw did not seem to warrant the
excitement: a few metal pieces in the shape of beans spread
out over a white cloth. Next day more excitement as Milos
discovered part of an earthenware relic filled with more of
the same metal objects. Both events were duly reported to the
governor, who immediately summoned Milos to a meeting.

The archaeologist appeared to sense that he might run into some
problems and, as a precaution, requested a Greek lawyer, Costa
Dafnides, to join him in the meeting. The governor wanted to

know what had been excavated so far. After some hesitation and consulting Dafnides, Milos produced his find of 22 metal beans. The governor's face dropped in amazement. He immediately recognized the objects as electrum coins of pure gold and silver coined in Ionia about 550 BC and of inestimable value to museums and private collectors. Some 10 years before, such coins had been found not far from the site of the recent discovery and even then they fetched £200,000 each.

The governor could not let the foreigners get away with such a huge fortune. There could well be several hundred electrums buried in the site and probably more in nearby locations. "I would like to cancel the lease-contract," suggested the governor, "and I would make it worth your while." Milos indicated that he had no intention of disposing of this "once-in-a-lifetime" bonanza at any price. However, after some sharp exchanges in Greek between the governor and the lawyer, Dafnides took Milos to one side and recommended a deal as the governor held all the aces in the form of the army who could make life intolerable for the lessee.

Eventually terms were agreed in the sum of £1 million. Milos could keep the coins he had found but had to vacate the site at once, leaving all the equipment behind. Furthermore, the parties agreed to a secrecy clause.

This extraordinary tale had an equally extraordinary sequel. On returning to London Milos handed the coins to an internationally known, very wealthy numismatist without payment and donated £200,000 to a charity.

Solve this intriguing puzzle!

THE THOROUGHBRED

Blithe Spirit, 10 times winner of the Grand National, is tied to a 30-foot rope. A haystack is 40 feet away. Nevertheless, the horse is able to eat the hay, even though the rope does not break or stretch in any way.

How is this possible?

THE BLIND MAN

A middle-aged man with dark glasses, a guide dog and white stick is walking slowly and carefully down the sidewalk of a very busy street in broad daylight. He has perfect eyesight, is not trying to beg, nor has he any criminal intent. What is he doing?

TIME IS OF THE ESSENCE

Ann Bassett is a light sleeper. She lives in apartment 5C on the fifth floor of a high-rise. Other tenants include many well-known names in industry, finance and the world of entertainment. Yvette Maynard, the actress, lived in 5A.

One November night Ann was woken by a scream and what she assumed was a gunshot. She hastily slipped onto a dressing gown and rushed out into the corridor. Just then, the door to 5A opened and a man rushed out. She recognized him as Johnny, Yvette's boyfriend. When he saw Ann he tried to hide his face, and when he passed her on his way to the fire escape he knocked her out with the gun in his hand. Just before she passed out, she observed the time showing on Yvette's grandfather clock, which she could just see through the open door. It was a quarter past midnight. Other tenants raised the alarm and Ann was taken to hospital by ambulance.

When Ann regained consciousness in the early hours of the morning, she was interviewed by the police. She proved an excellent witness. There was positive identification of the suspect, and she pinpointed the time of the crime. It was in fact murder, as Yvette had died instantly from a gunshot to her head. The police were, however, acutely disappointed when it transpired that the suspect had the best alibi one could imagine. John had been stopped in his car at precisely midnight for speeding. By the time he was allowed to drive on – after a breathalyzer test and taking particulars – it was almost 2 a.m.

As a precaution, the grandfather clock was checked and found to show the correct time. The case against Johnny had to be dropped. Yet Ann is convinced that he was the murderer, and she is right.

Can you solve the mystery?

ANSWERS

01 THE ASSASSIN

Eric was terminally ill and suffering intolerable pain. He had considered suicide, but the insurance policy on his life contained a suicide-exclusion clause. As Eric was determined to secure his family's financial future, he had hired a professional killer. His wife guessed what he had done and, for obvious reasons, did not want the killer to be apprehended.

02 BLUE EYES

The disaster mentioned in the puzzle was an accident in which Karen lost her sight. Ronnie was unable to cope with his wife's disability and left her.

After recovering from her traumatic experience she took the only job for which a blind person is eminently suitable, that of a switchboard operator. Karen was deeply attracted by Eric's voice and every time she heard him say 'Hello' it felt like a lover's kiss. However, when he wanted to meet her she realized the hopelessness of her situation, and rather than suffer the agony of another disappointment, she decided to withdraw.

03 THE LINE-UP

The photograph showed the six men in the line-up. One of them, answering the description, was coloured, dressed in a weird outfit, with a Mohican haircut and rings through his nose and left ear. The other five were white, well-dressed with pin-stripe trousers, dark jackets and ties, looking like typical professional men. Identity parade rules prescribe that all participants in a line-up should look reasonably alike.

04 THE BLUE MOVIE

Stephen was serious: he was head of the British Board of Film Censors.

05 WALKING TO THE PARK

Eric suffered from a compulsive obsession about cracks in the sidewalk; he would not step on them. To achieve this, he had to take exaggerated steps, which looked so odd. When he reached the park and could walk on the grass, his stride reverted to normal.

06 THE DIALOGUE

The piece of paper which the man presented to Elsa was a cash cheque. She recognized his signature and also the man's voice when he said 'No fifties.' 'How are you, Mr Wilson?' Elsa asked, to which he replied: 'I am frozen stiff, it is bitterly cold outside.'

Tom, overhearing the conversation, realized that the man was a customer and he withdrew.

07 MURDER IN THE FAMILY

William Garner knew right away which of his brothers-in-law had been murdered. Inspector Nelson had never specified which one was dead.

08 THE WEEKEND PARTY

Joan had put her contact lenses into a glass of water, which Fred swallowed without noticing. She was too short-sighted to drive and Fred had never driven. As there was no one else available to take the wheel, the rescue service had to help them out.

09 DRIVE CAREFULLY

The participants in this scenario were in the process of making a new James Bond film and the whole episode was staged.

10 LUXURY CRUISE

The Countess's necklace was in fact genuine and given to her by her rich lover. The Count had been told that the necklace was a well-made paste piece, which the Countess had bought herself. Gerrard knew that the piece was genuine but, seeing the expression on the face of the Countess, he guessed the situation and gallantly lied and paid the Count.

11 THE GLOBETROTTER

He is a postman who delivers letters to a number of embassies in London. The building and land of an embassy belong to the country concerned and are extra-territorial.

12 THE CONTRACTORS

The man was Pablo Picasso. The builder knew that the design in Picasso's own hand would be worth much more than the cost of constructing the extension.

13 ATTICA

Jaime had instantly realized, when Moses turned purple, that he was choking. He had first struck him on the back to try and dislodge the offending piece of food. When that failed, he had performed an emergency tracheotomy (opening the trachea, or windpipe, to provide a means of breathing when the natural air passage is obstructed above this level), thereby saving Moses' life.

14 THE COLLISION

There were only two vehicles involved in the collision. The vehicle which collided with Henry's was a transporter truck carrying a load of five cars.

15 THE PARROT

The parrot was deaf.

16 PILGRIMAGE

'Friday' was the donkey's name.

17 THE MURDER

They were filming a scene from a thriller and one of the two men on the terrace was a stuntman. When thrown from the building, he was supposed to fall into a safety net. The man in charge of the safety net had not rigged it properly, however, and the stuntman fell to his death. The man responsible for safety on the picture was charged with gross negligence.

18 THE ACCIDENT

The man had parachuted from a plane and become entangled in the tree.

19 HOMICIDE

Peter Collins was in fact a policeman. The trial had been a setup to enable him to gain the confidence of the Mafia contract killer and obtain evidence for a forthcoming Senate investigation.

20 THE MONEY CHANGERS

The operation was a well-planned scam. The sellers of the £50 notes were counterfeiters who had offered to sell 300,000 forged £50 notes at a discount of 60 per cent. The buyers wanted to be satisfied that the forged notes were of the highest quality and therefore arranged a pilot transaction. As the forgeries were of poor quality, the forgers used genuine notes as samples, and on bulk delivery they also used such notes on the top and bottom of each parcel. It is not known whether they got away with it.

21 THE JAMES DEAN APPRECIATION SOCIETY

The fans were watching the movie on a charter jet from New York to the venue of the society's national convention. suddenly the aircraft developed engine trouble in-flight and seemed about to crash when, just at the moment of the movie's sad climax, the pilot regained control.

22 THE LOVERS

The rain had started early the previous evening. When Inspector Jones arrived at Pamela's house, he noticed that the ground underneath Paul Johnson's car was dry, so it had obviously not been moved since the day before. Paul had in fact overheard the telephone conversation with Peter and he and Pamela had had a violent argument. Paul had flown into a jealous rage and clubbed Pamela to death with a candlestick. He then waited until morning to telephone the police with the fake story.

23 EYEWITNESS

Claire Vermont viewed the murder from outside the house. She had just arrived home after an evening out when she spotted her butler committing the murder in the living room.

24 THE VACANCY

Frank was having an affair with a young, married woman. She was the daughter of a diplomat born in Pakistan. Because she spoke Urdu and French, the advertisement fitted her like a glove. As her husband's salary was modest, he was more than happy to agree that his wife should accept this promising position, which enabled her to travel with her lover.

25 THE ICE-CREAM VENDOR

He told Ali: 'My name is Jaqua Ibn Aishaq. I am a Moslem myself. The ice cream I sell is awful, using cheap ingredients. While it's good enough for infidels, I am not going to sell to a nice Arab boy.'

26 THE INTERCOM

Thompson had forgotten that the master station was on loudspeaker unless you lifted the receiver.

27 THE SLIMMING PILL

As is the standard procedure in testing medication, half the group were given placebos (dummy pills used as controls). All participants in the test were encouraged to indulge, to demonstrate the effectiveness of the pill without dieting. The recipients of the placebo therefore gained weight.

28 LOST LUGGAGE

Alan Goide suddenly realized that the wrong suitcase had carried his name tag. This proved that the switch was deliberate, probably for the purpose of smuggling drugs.

29 THE STEELWORKER

David Edwin works the night shift at the steelworks and, as he lives in the basement of the high-rise, has to descend the stairs to reach his apartment.

30 THE INVENTION

This is a true story. A chain of bookmakers opening a new shop issued a tender for a telephone and loudspeaker system. Ollie's customer quoted low and won, installing Ollie's gadget. This had the effect that the running commentary of the race was received in the shop five minutes after the start. Punters belonging to the ring could listen to the broadcast through a Walkman and still place a bet when the race was sufficiently advanced, or indeed over, to identify the winning horse. This scam was used in the movie *The Sting* although there the scam was operated manually.

81 THE FIFTY-DOLLAR FIND

Since the same counterfeit note was used in all transactions, they are all invalid. But, realizing what had happened, the bank manager simply reimbursed the bank, saving the cleaning lady from being the sole loser. The manager did not really lose, as he had good value from the butcher, but the $50 find was wiped out.

82 THE HIJACK

The hijackers did not take the time to body-search their two victims, so they failed to notice that one had a cellular phone in the front pocket of his jacket. Despite the handcuffs, he managed, with the help of his co-worker, to get hold of the phone and dial 911. Speaking softly, he gave the police the truck's registration number and colour, and by looking out of a small window he was able to describe the route taken by the culprits.

83 THE BEACH

The island was the infamous Devil's Island. The man was a prisoner being rowed ashore by two prison guards. The main prison ship could only moor a quarter of a mile offshore because of treacherous reefs. During the journey the boat had been hit by a sudden squall and both guards were thrown overboard and drowned, whereas the prisoner, who was chained to the boat, had survived when the boat turned over, trapping an air pocket.

84 WHAT ARE THEY?

House numbers.

85 THE BURGLARS

John is 1 year old.

86 TWO-FINGER SALUTE

The men holding up two fingers were archers and they were indicating that the fingers

used to pull back the bowstrings were intact. (It was common practice in medieval times for prisoners of war to have their first two fingers cut off by their captors.)

87 THE PUNCTURES

The Mercedes was loaded on to the train.

88 THE ORCHARD

Bob Wilson lived on the 14th floor of a high-rise. The orchard consisted of miniature fruit trees planted in pots on his balcony. When he went out to pick fruit, he tripped and fell over the balcony, railing to his death below.

39 THE CEMETERY

This is essentially a true story, except for chronological inaccuracy.

During 1970, one Udo Proksch of Vienna founded an association promoting the idea that corpses should be buried in a vertical position. The project attracted many prominent proponents from all sections of Austrian society. In later years Proksch became notorious in connection with an insurance fraud which cost the life of six men. Udo Proksch was sentenced to life imprisonment and died in prison.

40 FOREIGN EXCHANGE

The director of the central bank, new in his position, had instructed the designer to mark the artist's drawing with the word 'Specimen'. As all the letters were in the Cyrillic alphabet, the printers failed to recognize this marking as a flaw.

Alerted to the 'problem', the printer pointed out to the bank that the notes would become collectors' items and would probably sell at more than their face value.

41 POOLS OF WATER

An organized street gang of youngsters had discovered an ingenious method to steal thousands of cigarettes, by freezing water into ice coins of a size which triggered the dispensing mechanism of the machines.

42 THE HUNDRED-DOLLAR NOTE

Steve devised a method whereby he used 14 $100 bills to make 15 bills (see diagram on previous page). He cut each of the notes into two parts very carefully. He then stuck the upper section (using clear adhesive tape) to the appropriate section of the next note with the result that 14 bills became 15.

Each note was, of course, shortened by one-fifteenth of its length, which was not normally noticeable. (This trick was actually tried in pre-war Austria.)

43 CELL PHONE

Poirot suggested to the stewardess that she ask the pilot to contact the control tower and request them to call Wolfgang's number. When his number rang in the first-class compartment the thief would be exposed.

44 HIT-AND-RUN

The defence failed. A professional taster never drinks even a drop of the wine he is sampling. He looks at it through light, smells it, swishes it around his mouth and then spits it out.

45 LOST

Bobby was a Labrador and John, his master, had used a dog whistle, inaudible to the human ear, to call him.

46 OVER THE LIMIT

The man was acting as a decoy to draw the policemen away from the club, whose members – some of whom were more than slightly inebriated – drove off in a hurry as soon as the coast was clear.

47 THE PEARL NECKLACE

'Harry Winston will be at the function and he knows an imitation if he sees one, so I had better take the real necklace from the bank vault.'

48 CIRCUMSTANTIAL EVIDENCE

Fred and Rona conspired to fake her disappearance, leaving sufficient clues behind to lead to Fred's arraignment. He was prepared to suffer a year in jail, hoping that on her reappearance he could file a substantial claim for wrongful arrest and imprisonment. The fact that she had left all her belongings behind, however, was sufficient proof of a conspiracy.

49 THE BLACK BOX

He is measuring the room with an Acutape, an instrument which registers the dimensions based on laser technology.

50 THE PILOT

Ara, on his day off, was flying a two-seater glider and had a comparatively soft crash landing.

51 THE EXPLORERS

The two men were deep-sea diving to explore the ocean floor for valuable minerals. They were diving to a depth of 100 metres, at which depth air in its natural proportion becomes dangerous.

During resurfacing, nitrogen bubbles can form in the diver's circulation (the bends), causing fatal blockages. To allow for safe decompression, the time for re-ascent can take hours. Several pioneers, including Arne Zetterstrom of Sweden, lost their lives by ascending too quickly.

52 THE SERIAL KILLER

US law enforcement agents are required by regulation to keep their working hand free. As it was easy to ascertain that both survivors were right-handed, the one whose right hand was free was in fact the Federal Agent.

53 D-DAY

The Procuring Office of the allied forces bought up all available inflatable life-sized dolls, which were then clad in uniforms disguised as paratroopers and dropped behind enemy lines north of Caen to disorientate the German defence.

54 THE PHONE RINGS

The meeting was a gathering of Mafia bosses. After welcoming the members, the overall boss told the meeting that one of them had broken the vow of OMERTA (absolute silence) and had betrayed them. He then pretended that a high-level contact at the police would shortly telephone and identify the traitor.

55 DAY OUT

The social club members were travelling to Northville by train, and Mr and Mrs Jones decided to go to the dining car at the rear of the train for a quick snack.

56 PLACE OF WORK

Norman is the navigator on a naval submarine, which has sunk in shallow waters a half mile out of port, on what was supposed to be a one-day test run. All rescue attempts have so far failed, as the escape hatch has jammed. He is alone, being the last surviving crew member, the others having drowned due to a leak. The food and water close at hand are fish and the sea. He can see the shore and several seafront restaurants through the periscope by which he is sitting.

57 DUSK OR DAWN?

Norman knew, of course, that the Amazon flows from west to east. It is also obvious that the sky at dawn is lighter in the east, and gradually darker toward the west, while at dusk the reverse is the case.

If he had had a watch he would have known instantly, as in the Brazilian winter (summer in the northern hemisphere) that the sun rises early in the morning and sets late in the evening.

58 THE RUNNER

Jonathan had actually lapped the Nigerian runner who, when he crossed the line, still had a lap to go, a fact which Jonathan almost immediately realized.

59 THE HELICOPTER

Single-rotor helicopters also have a small vertical tail rotor to counteract torque. Because of poor visibility I would have walked into the rotating tail rotor and been instantly killed. The two men realized that mere shouting would not have prevented the disaster and took the only possible action.

60 THE KEYS

Andrew hadn't told Raymond that he was travelling to Bristol for a few days. Therefore, Raymond had posted the keys to Andrew's Cambridge house, not realizing that they would be put through the mail slot in the door and that Andrew would then be unable to retrieve them in order to open the door.

61 THE SAWMILL

Boris was smuggling wheelbarrows.

62 DANGER IN THE AIR

The plane had landed at the airport but had not yet arrived at the terminal itself.

63 THE CRIME

Suicide!

64 THE MAQUIS

Jean-Claude was the assistant mayor of the town and as such had to have official contact with the Gestapo. He used his visits to headquarters to gather information useful to the Maquis. Georges was handed a gun with a dud bullet to test his total commitment to the cause.

65 THE JUDGEMENT

When the judge asked what long-eared owl tasted like, the man had replied, "The taste of the owl was a cross between a golden condor and a bald eagle." (Both are protected species.)

66 THE OPERATION

The man's son had been on a dialysis machine for years and his condition was deteriorating. Now his only partially working kidney was found to have a malignant growth and had to be removed. Although the doctors still hoped to find a suitable donor for a transplant, the father decided not to risk further delay.

67 THE CONTRACT

When Stephen telephoned Dave's answering machine he forgot to say what time it was when he phoned, making it impossible for Dave to know from what time the "40 minutes" started.

68 TABLE MANNERS

Lady Jane had dropped one of her contact lenses in the soup.

69 THE ASSASSIN

Tessino was shot in a drive-in cinema during a war scene.

70 THE BIRTHDAY PARTY

Albert's gift box contained chocolates with a note:

'Many happy returns, dear Joan, love Albert.'

Joan immediately realized that the bracelet and the loving note she had seen the day before were intended for Catherine, who was her twin sister.

71 THE CLAQUERS

Because of sudden illness of the leading actor, the French farce was replaced with a stand-by performance of Hamlet. The manager had failed to inform his crew of the programme change.

72 AVOIDING THE TRAIN

The man was walking through a train tunnel and was almost at the end when he heard a whistle and spotted the train coming toward him. He therefore had to move forward, toward the train, so that he could safely jump clear.

73 IN THE PARK

Sally was a Rottweiler bitch and the other dog was her mate.

74 THE SPY

The map showed the location of some real mines together with many non-existing ones, and thus hampered the war effort of the German navy. The document was deliberately played into the hands of the German spy.

75 PIT BULL TERRIER

Tom took one of his sausages and held it out of reach but within Kim's smelling distance. He began circling the tree with the dog following greedily until, after several revolutions, the leash winding around the tree became short enough, enabling Tom to retrieve his hat.

76 DEATH IN THE CAR

The man was in a convertible. He was shot when the top was down.

77 THE OPERATION

The nuclear scientist was a Canadian, who was operated on in Russia on the morning of 26 July. He died and was flown back to Canada to be cremated. The flight took him in an easterly direction over the international dateline, thus gaining a day.

78 THE KIDNAP

Dr Bernstein had an enlargement done of the photograph and managed to decipher the address of the recipient of the newspaper which had been written by the newsagent in the top corner of the front page.

79 THE HEIR

The test was a blood test. The elder knew that the true prince was in fact a haemophiliac.

80 ACCIDENT PRONE

When Steve fell the first time, the concrete forecourt had only just been laid and was still wet. The soft cement acted as a cushion. By the time the second fall occurred the concrete had set hard, thereby causing multiple fractures.

81 THE SUSPECT

Brian devised what he considered a foolproof plan to cover his tracks. He had taped his conversation with Clifford on a previous afternoon visit with a tape recorder hidden in his briefcase. After killing Clifford, he played the recording as he left the study for the benefit of his uncle's housekeeper.

On re-reading her testimony, the housekeeper suddenly realized that she had heard the grandfather clock chime six when the time was actually 11 p.m.

82 THE STAGECOACH ROBBERY

When Billy arrived at the log cabin it had only just started to snow. He stabled his horse and entered the empty cabin in search of food and drink. By the time he finished eating, it had stopped snowing but there was a thick blanket of snow on the ground.

Suddenly the Kid had a flash of inspiration. His plan to trick the posse, which no doubt was after him, seemed foolproof. He walked backwards from the cabin to the stables, and fixed new shoes on top of his horse's old ones but in reverse. He then rode his horse from the stables and headed north. The posse saw these tracks, followed them to the stables and cabin, but did not understand how their quarry could possibly have escaped.

83 THE TUNNEL

Bob was so exasperated by the uncouth behaviour of Heinz Klausner that he grasped the opportunity of the blackout to imitate a kiss as a prelude to punching the German.

84 THE LONER

John was in a cinema on 5th Avenue, which was showing a newsreel of the assassination attempt on the President. When the incident was shown, John had fired two shots at the screen.

85 THE ACCIDENT

Tracy was Scott's sister, and as he was covered by third party insurance, and as they had agreed to share the proceeds, they were both in pocket.

86 A SAFE PLACE

(a) Playing baseball.

(b) Catcher.

(c) Third base.

87 THE FANCY-DRESS BALL

The date was the 1st of April, and Martin was the victim of a practical joke. His colleagues in the mail room had Martin's invitation specially printed, referring to a fancy-dress party, while all others specified "formal dress."

88 THE SYSTEM

Frank and Johnny were trying to launder drug money. One of the two would very likely show a substantial win at the end of the session, which would legitimate the cash he got for the chips. The compensating loss by his partner would go unnoticed. It is true that over a period of time the partnership would lose a small amount, about 1.35 per cent on the combined turnover, but in the long run the scheme would probably turn out cheaper – and certainly safer – than laundering through conventional channels.

89 THE NEWSPAPER

Sisters Lisa and Joan occupied adjoining rooms in their home. The connecting door had been locked by the mother to stop the girls from chatting at night. Lisa had slid half of the newspaper under the door.

90 VICTORIA STATION

Brian was a bus driver. Bill was running to catch the bus, which he did, and thereafter became a passenger.

91 DEVOTED COUPLE

James knew that he was suffering from a terminal illness and had decided to commit suicide, firstly to spare his wife having to look after him as his illness became worse, and secondly so that she would receive full insurance to provide for her needs. He therefore staged his own murder as the insurance policy had a suicide-exclusion clause. He had locked the study door, opened the window, started a conversation with an imaginary visitor as soon as he heard his wife try the door handle and then stabbed himself, using the cloth which he had been using to clean his trophies to keep the knife clear of fingerprints. The cloth had fallen to the floor after he stabbed himself.

92 THE BIRTHDAY

Alice had a wealthy boyfriend who wanted to buy her an expensive birthday present. They had shopped together and selected a costly bracelet, but as this would have been difficult for Alice to explain to her husband, she and her boyfriend conspired with the jeweller to go along with the deception and quote George a much lower price.

93 THE ARCHAEOLOGIST

Milos Sudsic had a close friend, a very rich numismatist, who agreed to lend him part of his collection of electrums on the understanding that Milos would make a very generous donation to charity. Milos had devized a scam in which he would plant the borrowed coins on the Greek site and then pretend to find them. On his return to England he returned the coins to his collector friend, made a payment of £200,000 to charity, then pocketed the substantial balance.

94 THE THOROUGHBRED

The other end of the rope isn't attached to anything.

95 THE BLIND MAN

He is an actor rehearsing a scene for the starring role in a TV series about a blind detective.

96 TIME IS OF THE ESSENCE

Ann was right. Johnny had committed the crime. But how could she have mistaken the time? What she saw through the open door was the clock's image in a mirror covering one of the walls. The reflection reversed the time shown on the clock – a quarter to twelve – to read 12.15.

ACKNOWLEDGEMENTS

Sources for this type of puzzle are relatively rare and offer insufficient material to fill a book of this size. Consequently many "Strange Situations" had to be invented and I spent many sleepless nights racking my brains. I also became a scourge to friends and relatives cajoling them to contribute.

The response was less than overwhelming, though I should be grateful for small mercies. In addition, I am indebted to the following authors and/or publishers whose material I have used in its original form, or whose ideas have provided me with raw material for some of the "Hidden Evidence" stories I have constructed: Victor Serebriakoff – *A Mensa Puzzle Book*; Scot Morris – *Omni Games*; Martin Gardner; P. Carter & K. Russell; Eugene P. Northrop; and Gyles Brandreth.

Les Smith assisted in producing original ideas and being the devil's advocate in criticizing puzzles of my own construction. Jennifer Iles coped most efficiently with numerous changes and revisions.